FASHION PHOTOGRAPHY

By John Hamilton

Abdo & Daughters
An imprint of Abdo Publishing | abdopublishing.com

abdopublishing.com

Published by Abdo Publishing, a division of ABDO, PO Box 398166, Minneapolis, Minnesota 55439. Copyright © 2019 by Abdo Consulting Group, Inc. International copyrights reserved in all countries. No part of this book may be reproduced in any form without written permission from the publisher. Abdo & Daughters™ is a trademark and logo of Abdo Publishing.

Printed in the United States of America, North Mankato, Minnesota.
082018
092018

THIS BOOK CONTAINS RECYCLED MATERIALS

Editor: Sue Hamilton
Copy Editor: Bridget O'Brien
Graphic Design: Sue Hamilton
Cover Design: Candice Keimig and Pakou Moua
Cover Photos: iStock
Interior Images: Eastman-Kodak-pg 8 (top); Fujifilm North America-pg 13; iStock-pgs 4, 5, 6, 9, 11 (top), 12, 14, 15, 16, 17 (top), 18 (top), 19, 20 (top), 21, 22, 24, 25, 26, 27, 28, 29, 30, 31, 32, 33, 34, 35, 40, 41, 42, 43, 44 & 45 (top);
John Hamilton-pg 18 (bottom); Nikon USA-pgs 9 (inset), 10, 14 (inset), 15 (inset), 16 (inset), 17 (inset) & 20 (bottom); Shutterstock-pgs 7, 8 (bottom), 11 (bottom), 17 (bottom), 23, 36-37, 38 & 39; U.S. Copyright Office-pg 45 (bottom).

Library of Congress Control Number: 2017963908
Publisher's Cataloging-in-Publication Data
Names: Hamilton, John, author.
Title: Fashion photography / by John Hamilton.
Description: Minneapolis, Minnesota : Abdo Publishing, 2019. | Series: Digital photography | Includes online resources and index.
Identifiers: ISBN 9781532115868 (lib.bdg.) | ISBN 9781532156793 (ebook)
Subjects: LCSH: Fashion photography--Juvenile literature. | Fashion prints--Juvenile literature. | Fashion in art--Juvenile literature. | Photography--Digital techniques--Juvenile literature.
Classification: DDC 778.9939--dc23

CONTENTS

FASHION IMAGES

One of the highest-paying and most sought-after jobs in photography is fashion. Fashion photography is about selling clothing, of course. But it also celebrates a lifestyle, the dream of wearing current and exciting apparel. Fashion photographers create a mood. It is a chance to let their creativity shine.

Professional fashion photographers are part of a team. They work with models who show off fabulous clothing lines. They also have a crew of people who share their skills, including clothing stylists, hair stylists, makeup artists, and lighting assistants. When you are just starting out, you will probably handle many of these jobs yourself. The road to success can be difficult, but it is always exciting and fun if you love creating your own style.

Professionals work as a team to get the desired fashion photograph.

EDITORIAL FASHION PHOTOGRAPHY

There are many kinds of fashion photography. They fall into two main groups: editorial and commercial. Editorial fashion photography appears mostly in magazines, newspapers, and online. Often shot on location, editorial photos usually accompany a written story that reflects an idea or lifestyle. The photos and wardrobes are tied together in some way. For example, an editorial photo shoot might feature a collection of colorful tops, or the newest swimwear, but not usually both. Models aren't as posed in editorial photos. They act out the story while showcasing the fashions.

COMMERCIAL FASHION

HIGH FASHION

Commercial fashion photography sells a brand or collection of clothing. In catalogues, clear images and simple backgrounds are used to show off the product. The models' poses are toned down. The attention is on the product being sold, either clothing, jewelry, makeup, or accessories.

High fashion is a kind of commercial fashion photography where creativity runs wild. Wardrobe styling is dramatic, like a living fantasy. Models pose in exaggerated ways. Their faces are often calm, but sometimes are filled with raw emotion. Hair, makeup, and lighting are almost theatrical, working together to bring the photographer's vision and creativity to life.

CAMERAS

Digital photography captures a scene when light passes through a lens and is focused onto an image sensor. The sensor converts the light into digital form. It is then stored as a file that can be transferred to a computer for later processing. The first portable digital camera was made by Eastman Kodak in 1975. It weighed eight pounds (3.6 kg) and shot only in black-and-white. Digital cameras as we know them today first became popular in the 1990s and early 2000s.

The first portable digital camera was made by Steven Sasson for Eastman Kodak in 1975.

Most fashion photography today is done digitally because of the many advantages over film. One of the best parts is seeing your photos right away so you can change settings if needed. Also, you can take hundreds of shots on a single memory card. No more missed shots while changing film cartridges!

Digital cameras allow you to check your photos and change settings if needed.

With a DSLR (Digital Single Lens Reflex) camera, you can look through the viewfinder or use the camera's screen display to see exactly what you're shooting.

Most professional fashion photographers today use DSLR (Digital Single Lens Reflex) cameras. With a DSLR, you actually peer through the camera lens so you can see exactly what you're shooting. Angle of view and sharpness are determined by the lens. DSLR lenses are "interchangeable," which means you can change one lens for another depending on your creative needs.

When light travels inside the DSLR, it is diverted by a mirror into a glass prism. It directs the light into the viewfinder. When you press the shutter release button, this "reflex" mirror flips up and the shutter behind it opens. Light strikes the image processor. After the exposure, the shutter closes, and the mirror flips back down.

The image sensor inside the camera has millions of light-capturing pixels that record an image. The greater the number of pixels, the higher the resolution of the picture. A 20-megapixel (20-million-pixel) sensor almost always has a better resolution than a 10-megapixel sensor. Modern DSLR sensors usually come equipped with at least 16 to 24 megapixels. The size of the image sensor is also important. The large sensors in many DSLRs produce the most detailed pictures, and they can capture images in low light without too much digital noise ruining the scene.

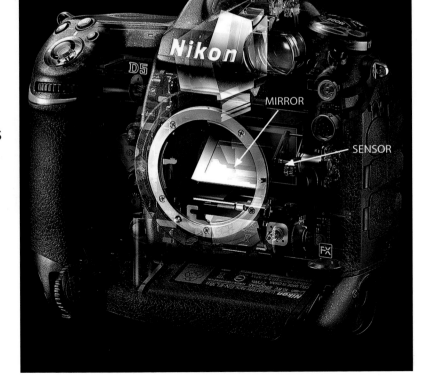

The inside workings of a DSLR camera.

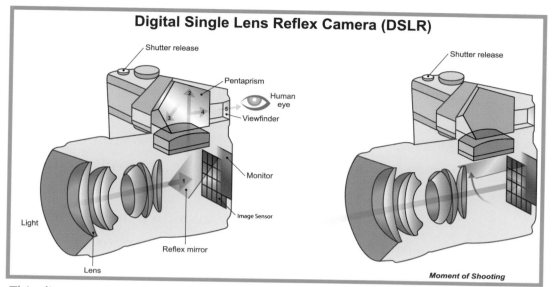

Digital Single Lens Reflex Camera (DSLR)

Shutter release
Pentaprism
Human eye
Viewfinder
Monitor
Image Sensor
Reflex mirror
Light
Lens

Shutter release
Moment of Shooting

This diagram shows how a DSLR camera creates a photograph.

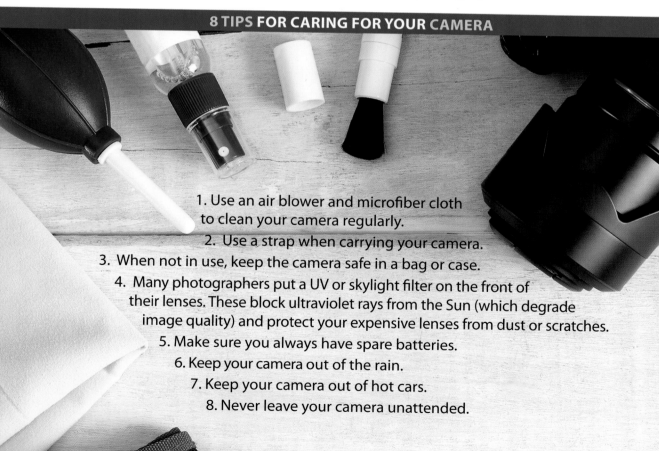

8 TIPS FOR CARING FOR YOUR CAMERA

1. Use an air blower and microfiber cloth to clean your camera regularly.
2. Use a strap when carrying your camera.
3. When not in use, keep the camera safe in a bag or case.
4. Many photographers put a UV or skylight filter on the front of their lenses. These block ultraviolet rays from the Sun (which degrade image quality) and protect your expensive lenses from dust or scratches.
5. Make sure you always have spare batteries.
6. Keep your camera out of the rain.
7. Keep your camera out of hot cars.
8. Never leave your camera unattended.

A cell phone is sometimes used as a primary or backup camera.

There is an old saying that the best camera is the one you have on you. For many people, especially those just starting out, that means a cell phone. The image quality of most cell phones has greatly improved in recent years. Most professional photographers carry one as a backup. Cell phones automatically focus and adjust exposure. Many allow you to manually override these settings for creative effects. Some even have dual lenses that let you simulate a shallow depth of field. This throws the background out of focus while keeping the subject sharp for a pleasing portrait effect.

Cell phone cameras do have disadvantages. It usually takes longer to set up a shot than with a DSLR. Adjusting exposure with an app and attaching a clip-on lens can be awkward. In addition, cell phone cameras are tricky in low-light situations. Be sure to hold it steady, or even use a tripod with a special mount, to avoid blurry photos.

Mirrorless cameras are becoming more popular each year. Like DSLRs, different lenses can be mounted on most of them (some have fixed lenses). However, there is no mirror or glass prism. This makes mirrorless cameras lightweight and quiet to shoot. Yet, they have excellent image quality, even in low light.

If you are a beginner, don't worry too much about which camera to buy. Think about what you want to do with it and which features are important to you. Amazing images can be taken with almost all digital cameras sold today. The truth is, it's the creative mind behind the camera that matters most.

A mirrorless camera produced by Fujifilm. This type of camera is lightweight and quiet to shoot, yet produces excellent image quality, even in low light.

LENSES

J ust as important as your camera are the lenses you use. They determine the "field of view" of your scene. A wide-angle lens shows more of the surrounding area. A telephoto lens captures just a small part, which is why everything looks magnified.

A lens's field of view is measured in millimeters. A "normal" field of view captured by a full-frame image sensor is about 50mm. That is about the same as what you perceive with your eyes. Common wide-angle lenses are about 24mm to 35mm. Super-wide lenses start at about 10mm. Below that are fisheye lenses, which are used for special effects because of their distortion.

Fisheye lenses cause distortion that bends straight lines.

A 24-70mm zoom is a flexible lens for shooting in a studio or on location.

Most fashion photographers own at least one wide-angle lens. They make it easy to photograph lifestyle group shots, and full-body shots where you also want to show the background. They have a very wide range of focus, or "depth of field." Despite these advantages, wide-angle lenses below about 35mm aren't often used in fashion photography. The distortion they create is unflattering, although they can occasionally be used creatively.

FILTERS

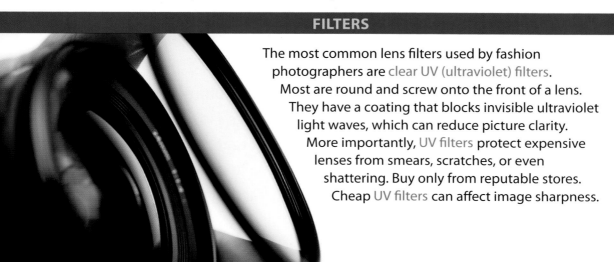

The most common lens filters used by fashion photographers are clear UV (ultraviolet) filters. Most are round and screw onto the front of a lens. They have a coating that blocks invisible ultraviolet light waves, which can reduce picture clarity. More importantly, UV filters protect expensive lenses from smears, scratches, or even shattering. Buy only from reputable stores. Cheap UV filters can affect image sharpness.

A sharp, lightweight 50mm lens is good for many kinds of fashion shots.

When you start shooting fashion, you might only own the 50mm lens that came with your camera. These lenses are actually preferred by many fashion photographers. They are sharp and lightweight, great for full-length body shots that show off clothes, and for waist-up portraits. They cause little distortion. Many have very wide apertures, as low as f/1.4 on some lenses. That produces just a sliver of depth of field, with the model's face in sharp focus and everything else turned into a pleasing background blur. Some photographers carry a zoom lens that includes a range of medium focal lengths, such as a 24-70mm zoom.

Moderate telephotos range from about 80 to 200mm. They create a pleasing compression effect in the models' faces. Noses and other facial features seem to flatten out slightly. This creates a very flattering look that most people like. Long lenses also make it easier to shoot with a shallow depth of field, which blurs distracting backgrounds.

A 70-210mm zoom is an excellent overall lens that flattens facial features and can blur the background.

There is no "best" lens for fashion. Each focal length has its advantages and disadvantages. Sharpness and the ability to shoot with wide apertures is important. As you learn and grow as a photographer, you'll add to your collection of "glass." The most important thing is to invest in the highest-quality lenses you can afford. They should last you a lifetime.

LENS HOODS

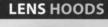

Lens Hood →

Lens hoods are plastic (usually) extensions that fit onto the front of your lens. They keep Sun flare from washing out your photos. They can also protect your expensive lens's front glass element from bumps and scratches.

EXPOSURE

A camera's shutter-speed dial.

Exposure is the amount of light that strikes the camera's image sensor. Three settings determine the "correct" exposure. They include ISO, shutter speed, and aperture. All three work together.

ISO is the image sensor's sensitivity to light. If you double the ISO, you make the sensor twice as sensitive. However, more digital noise is then created. The lower the ISO, the better the quality. For example, when shooting in bright sunlight, you would normally set an ISO of 100 or 200. However, in dim scenes, you might increase it to 800 or more. Otherwise, your exposures would be so long that you couldn't hold your camera steady enough to avoid blurring (camera shake). Blurring can also occur if your subject moves during long exposures.

This photograph shows noticeable camera shake. It is very apparent in the subject's eyes.

In this image the shutter speed was increased from 1/40 to 1/125 second. The subject is much sharper.

Choosing the right exposure for a fashion shoot is a balance between areas of light and dark (tone) and focus (depth of field). These are controlled by shutter speed and aperture.

Shutter speed is the length of time the camera's shutter opens to let light strike the image sensor. It is measured in seconds (usually a fraction of a second). Each setting is twice as long, or half as short, as the setting next to it. Shutter speeds must be fairly fast to avoid camera shake, usually in the range of 1/125 to 1/250 second. Wide-angle lenses can be used with slower shutter speeds.

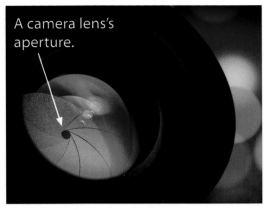
A camera lens's aperture.

Lenses have apertures, or holes, in the back where they are mounted to the camera. Apertures can be adjusted much like the irises in your eyes. They are measured in "f-stops." The smaller the f-stop number, the more light is allowed into the camera.

The important thing to remember is that if you increase one setting, such as shutter speed, then you must reduce the other setting (aperture) in order to get back to your original exposure.

When you are starting out, it's okay to put your camera on automatic. DSLRs have a setting on the exposure dial called "P," which stands for program mode. Modern cameras are like small computers. They examine the scene and figure out the math for you. The camera will pick a shutter speed and aperture combination. This will allow you to concentrate on other things, like focus and composition.

The exposure dial is set at "P" for program mode.

Large Depth of Field-Sharp Overall

Fashion shots with high-end jewelry need to be sharp. Try an aperture of f/8 or f/11.

Shallow Depth of Field-Eyes Sharp

For a shallow depth of field effect, try f/2.8 or wider. Get close to the model and focus on the eye nearest the camera.

As you get more practice taking pictures, you'll soon want to control these settings yourself in creative ways. For example, controlling the aperture also controls the amount of depth of field in your scene. That means you have control over what is in sharp focus.

Typical lens f-stop settings.

GETTING A STEADY SHOT

To properly handhold your camera, make sure your elbows are tucked in near your body. The camera should rest in the palm of your hand. Gently squeeze the shutter release. Don't stab at it with your finger. These steps will help you get a steady shot.

When you handhold your camera, pictures can get blurry during long exposures. This is especially true when light levels are dim, such as at dusk, or in a wooded park or dark alley. When you take portraits in natural light, you might need extra support to avoid camera shake.

If there's one piece of equipment every photographer should own, it's a sturdy tripod. You simply cannot handhold your camera in dim light and expect sharp results, especially with a telephoto lens. You can raise your camera's ISO to make it more sensitive to light, but that reduces quality by increasing digital noise.

Tripods come in many shapes and sizes, and some can be very expensive. In general, the best tripods are heavy (to give your camera a solid platform), made of metal or carbon fiber, and have adjustable-length tubular legs.

Tripods give your camera a solid platform.

If you shoot in a studio or on location using artificial light, you might not need to use a tripod. Flash and continuous studio lights (either incandescent, fluorescent, or LED) usually provide enough illumination to handhold your camera without worrying about camera shake. Many studio photographers like to handhold their camera so they can move around the set more easily. Others prefer using a tripod. Once the camera is set up, they can concentrate on directing the model.

BEST SHUTTER SPEED FOR HANDHOLDING THE CAMERA

If you're handholding your camera, how do you know if the shutter speed is fast enough to create a sharp image? The rule of thumb is to shoot at a shutter speed higher than the reciprocal of the focal length of your lens. In other words, if you're shooting with a 200mm lens, you'll need a shutter speed of at least 1/200 second in order to get a sharp picture. If you're shooting with a wide-angle 24mm lens, you can go all the way down to 1/24 second. If you set your camera to "Program" or "Auto," it will calculate this for you.

Natural Lines

Good composition uses natural lines (leading lines) to draw the viewer's eye to the subject.

COMPOSITION

Fashion photographers use composition to guide the viewer's eye to the main subject in the photo. You don't need expensive equipment or exotic locations to make stunning images. Composition is all about arranging the scene in your viewfinder in the best way to tell your story.

Good composition uses many artistic elements. They include color, contrast, texture, framing, and natural lines. You can use all of these things to lead the viewer's eye to your subject. If the model takes up just a small part of the frame, use natural lines (also called leading lines) in the background or foreground to draw the eye to the subject.

Backgrounds can help or hurt your composition. Sometimes a busy background will give context to your scene. Other times, it distracts from the person you're photographing. Before taking a photo, check to be sure things like poles or pillars aren't growing out of the head of your subjects. Large apertures, such as f/2.8 on some lenses, will blur the background, hiding much of the clutter.

THE RULE OF THIRDS

Many fashion shots have their subjects in the center of the photograph. There is nothing wrong with this, especially if you're filling the frame with a person's face. Sometimes, however, you may want to be more creative with your compositions, especially if you're including the background. The "rule of thirds" is a way of dividing the viewfinder into three horizontal parts and three vertical parts. Instead of a "rule," think of it as a helpful guideline. Oftentimes, putting your subject off-center makes the composition more pleasing and interesting.

WORKING WITH NATURAL LIGHT

Depending on the time of day, natural sunlight may be all you need to create professional-quality photographs. The light can be edgy and hard, or diffused and soft, depending on how you use it. During early morning or at dusk (the "golden hour") the Sun gives off a wonderful, warm light. If you angle the model to the side, the direct side lighting brings out textures (best for male models). If clouds cover the Sun, the overcast light is diffused, with fewer shadows.

Golden Hour	**Side Light**	**Overcast Light**
At dawn or dusk the Sun gives off a wonderful warm light.	To see textures, put light on one side and shadows on the other.	If clouds cover the Sun, the light is diffused and fewer shadows are seen.

OPEN SHADE

During the light of the midday Sun, people's skin appears shiny. Hot spots show up as featureless white blobs. Shadows create dark patches under the eyes. Instead of shooting in direct sunlight, move your subject to a shady spot that blocks the Sun, such as under a tree or a roof awning. This "open shade" softens and diffuses the harsh light of the Sun. Open your lens up wide, to f/2.8 for example. This will give you a fast shutter speed, allowing you to handhold without camera shake. It will also throw the background out of focus. This separation between the background and the sharp foreground will make your subject the center of attention.

BACKLIGHTING

Backlighting means putting your light source—the Sun—directly behind your model. The Sun itself doesn't necessarily appear in the frame, although that can result in very dramatic and trendy photos. Backlighting creates a halo around your subject, and hair seems to glow.

If you just take a quick picture with the Sun behind your subject, you'll get a silhouette. Instead, first use your camera's meter and aim at your model's face. That tells the camera to expose for your subject instead of the bright background. Lock in the exposure (see your camera's manual for instructions) and start shooting. It may take a few tries, but the results make it worth the effort.

WINDOW LIGHT

Photographing with natural light doesn't mean you always have to shoot outdoors. One of the best tools at a photographer's disposal is sunlight pouring in from a large window. The light can be very soft and diffused or directional and dramatic. For contrasty hard light, have your subject stand next to the window, maybe gazing outside as if in deep thought.

For a softer look, you need to diffuse the light streaming through the window. This is especially nice light when photographing models. Attach a white bed sheet, or even a frosted vinyl shower curtain, over the window. This diffuses the light, spreading it out to softly wrap around the model.

REFLECTORS

Reflectors are invaluable tools, especially when shooting in natural light. In many cases, sunlight will produce too many dark shadows. The dark areas are very apparent on faces and in the folds on some outfits. To fill in the shadows, bounce some of the sunshine back into your model with a large reflector.

Professional reflectors are usually made of a shiny fabric stretched across a round- or rectangular-shaped frame that is often foldable. You can make your own with white cardboard. You can also buy large sheets of a type of light, white-colored material called foam core at your local craft or hardware store.

Have an assistant get close to the model without being in the picture. Then use the reflector to bounce sunlight back into his or her face. Angle the reflector until the light fills in the shadows for a more pleasing look. Some reflectors have a gold coating on one side that warms up the model's skin, mimicking dawn or dusk light.

A reflector is used to bounce sunlight back onto a model's face. This helps fill in the shadows and creates a more pleasing look.

A model is photographed using natural sunlight and a reflector.

If you're photographing models in open shade, try bouncing light from a reflector into their faces. This will give them even more separation from the background, and produce a beautiful even light. This method works even better with heavy backlighting from the Sun. Many professional-quality fashion shots are taken with nothing more than natural sunlight and a reflector.

STUDIO LIGHTING

Sometimes sunlight isn't available, or you want more control when lighting your models. In many cases, you can't risk bad weather during a shoot, which would ruin hair and clothing. In these cases, it's best to shoot inside a photo studio using artificial light sources.

There are many tools to create and control artificial light. Flash units, also called strobes, create a brief burst of light. They range from large, powerful units used in professional photo studios, to small strobes (often called speedlights) that can be handheld, mounted on a stand, or attached to a hotshoe bracket on top of the camera.

When fired directly on top of the camera, strobes give off an even, harsh light. They can also cause the dreaded red-eye effect in your subjects. For best results, use one or more wireless-controlled flash units off-camera to sculpt the light for creative effects. Entire books and websites are devoted to this subject. They include excellent tutorials by professional photographers such as Scott Kelby, Joe McNally, and David Hobby.

Flash/Strobe

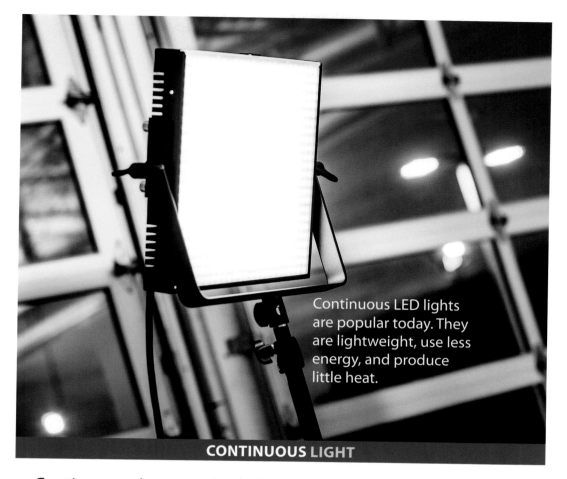

Continuous LED lights are popular today. They are lightweight, use less energy, and produce little heat.

CONTINUOUS LIGHT

Continuous photographic light sources provide a steady stream of illumination. Their biggest advantage is that you can see exactly the effect you want before you press the shutter button. However, they're not as portable as small flash units, and they can heat up a studio very quickly. But unlike strobes, continuous lights can double as lights used for video production.

Continuous lights are often called studio lights, or hot lights. They mainly use bright tungsten or fluorescent bulbs. In recent years, LED lights have become very popular. They are lightweight, use less energy, and produce little heat.

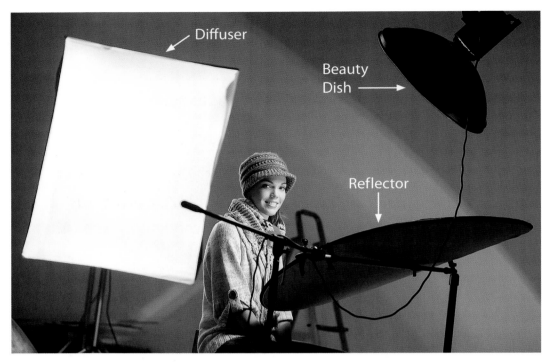

Diffuser

Beauty Dish →

Reflector

A combination of light modifiers, such as a reflector and a diffuser, help photographers control how a subject is illuminated.

LIGHT MODIFIERS

Besides reflectors, there are many other kinds of tools that you can use to creatively modify how light looks on your subjects. Diffusers are semi-transparent sheets of material. They spread, or "diffuse," hard directional light. You place diffusers between the subject and the Sun, a strobe, or other artificial light source. Diffusers create a soft, glowing effect that is very pleasing for fashion. You can make them yourself using materials such as white bed sheets or frosted shower curtains.

A beauty dish is a round, bowl-shaped light modifier, usually with a white or silver lining. Light from a flash is directed into the dish, and then reflected onto the model. Often used for head-and-shoulders fashion shots, the light is direct, dramatic, and wraps around the model's face.

Photographic umbrellas are inexpensive light modifying tools. A strobe or continuous light source is mounted to a stand, and then the umbrella is attached. The light bounces off the umbrella's reflective surface and spreads out. The resulting light is softer, creating an even quality that fills in shadows. It works especially well when placed very close to the subject.

Softboxes are similar to umbrellas, but the light is contained inside a fabric enclosure. Light escapes through a cloth diffusion panel on one side. Softboxes create a narrower beam of light than umbrellas. That makes the light more controllable. However, they are more expensive and difficult to set up.

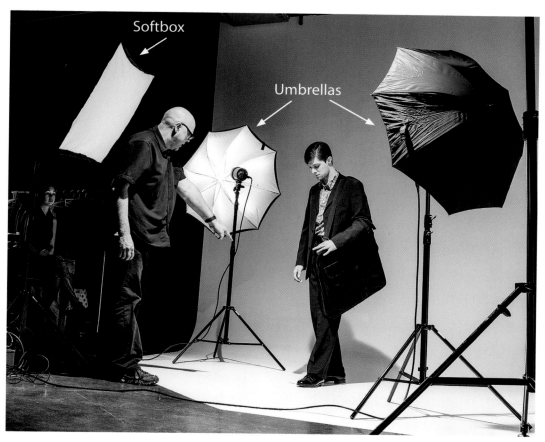

WORKING WITH MODELS

The models who pose in your fashion photos may be professionals or simply friends who want a fun experience. Either way, there are things you can do to make the shoot more enjoyable for everyone, which will result in better pictures for you.

First, make sure the models understand your project. Share your vision and make them your partners. Be specific. Give instructions like, "I'm looking for fun and bright photos, not dark and brooding."

Don't put the models in dangerous situations, like asking them to pose in the middle of a street or on slippery rocks at the edge of a lake. Don't touch the models without permission, and don't refer to their bodies in offensive ways. Always be respectful and polite.

Be positive and professional when working with models. Give general directions and start shooting. If a different pose is needed, tell them what *is* working *first*. Then say what *both* of you can do to make it better.

As you shoot, give your models positive feedback. Compliment them, and be sure to show them the good shots you're taking. With encouragement, they will loosen up and be more expressive in their posing. If something goes wrong with your camera settings or lighting, don't grumble and get angry. The models will think they're to blame, and will only stiffen up. Stay positive and motivate them.

Don't over-direct your models. Give them general directions for what you want, and keep it simple. Guide them, but don't treat them like mannequins. When you create the right atmosphere, trust them to come up with their own poses. If you need to nudge things along, try having them act out a scene or emotion. Always talk and give compliments, and be ready to capture the magic with your camera.

If you make your models comfortable, and make them feel like they're partners in your creative vision, you will connect with them. That trust and energy will translate into better poses and better pictures, not to mention more fun. If the shoot goes well, your models will want to work with you again and again.

8 WAYS **TO MAKE** YOUR **MODELS** COMFORTABLE

1. Discuss the shoot beforehand so the models understand the theme.
2. Compliment and encourage them.
3. Give the models general directions and let them "do their thing." Don't over-direct.
4. Find out what kind of music your models enjoy, and play it during the session.
5. Talk to the models, find out what they like. Be friendly, but professional.
6. Show the models how the images are turning out.
7. Have food and drinks available.
8. Take regular breaks, especially if it's a long session.

STREET LOCATIONS

You don't need an expensive studio or exotic locations to take great fashion shots. Awesome backgrounds can be found almost anywhere. You might have all the backgrounds you need right in your own neighborhood.

CARS

Cars and trucks can be found parked almost everywhere. They can make a great painterly background if you find one with colors

that compliment your model's outfit, hair, or skin. Have the model take several steps away from the car. Use a long lens (such as 200mm) and a wide-open aperture, such as f/2.8. The shallow depth of field results in beautiful textures and colors behind the model.

WALLS

Walls can make great backgrounds, especially stone and brick. Models can stand out nicely against the textures and colors found in stone walls. One shooting method is to have the model stand sideways against the wall. Use a telephoto lens and a wide aperture for a small depth of field. This will blur out the stone that recedes in the background.

USE YOUR BACKGROUND LANDSCAPE

If you find a scene that has beautiful elements, such as a cityscape, mountain, or beach, use it in your photo. Put a medium-length lens on your camera (such as 50mm). Open the aperture wide (such as f/2.8). The background will be visible, but blurred slightly so the model is still the center of attention.

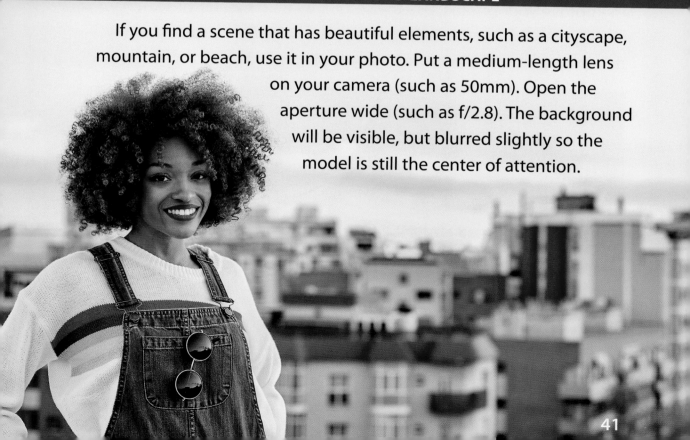

THE DIGITAL DARKROOM

Photos taken with modern cameras are usually well exposed and in focus, but there's always room for improvement. That's where the digital darkroom comes in. Fixing a photo's range of tones (its light and dark pixels) can improve it dramatically. Color balance, sharpening, and cropping are also common enhancements. These are all easy to perform with modern digital photo software, such as Photoshop, Lightroom, or GIMP. There are even inexpensive apps for cell phones that let you experiment with your photos.

Image editing software can be difficult to learn, but it is a fun way to improve your photos. Use the software's help menus, or search for online video instructions. Everyone was a beginner once, and many generous photographers are happy to share their skills.

Postproduction work can dramatically enhance a photo.

Almost every photo can be made better with image processing software such as Photoshop or Lightroom. In the above photo, the colors were warmed up to counter the bluish cast caused by the mid-day Sun. Overall vibrance and contrast were boosted, and a dark vignette circled the image to draw attention to the model.

BACKING UP YOUR PHOTOS

Make copies of your digital images. Keep them safe on at least two storage devices. All hard drives will fail eventually. Without a backup, your photos will vanish, representing many months, perhaps years, of hard work.

In most professional studios, photos are backed up on several different devices. In addition to the hard drive on your main computer, use backup software every day to automatically copy all your photos onto a portable hard drive. These small devices get cheaper every year, with bigger capacities. Every few days or weeks, swap out the external drive with one that you might keep in a safe deposit box at your bank. This strategy is called having an off-site backup. If disaster strikes, such as your house burning down or washing away in a flood, your work will remain safe.

Portable hard drives hold a lot of photos and can be kept in different locations as off-site backups.

PORTABLE
HARD DRIVE

A USB flash drive is an easy and portable way to back up your photographs. It is a good device to use when traveling.

If you're just starting out, you don't need to rent a safe deposit box. Store your off-site backup at a friend or relative's house for safekeeping. You'll be glad you did if your files are ever damaged.

Some photographers store off-site backups in the Cloud. That means using the Internet to automatically store digital copies on large computer servers run by companies such as Dropbox, Apple, or Google. Cloud storage can be impractical because digital photo collections often grow to many gigabytes in size and could take days to upload. However, technology changes rapidly, and Cloud storage becomes more appealing with each passing year.

For extra protection, you can also keep your best files backed up on USB flash drives. After copying, toss them in a desk drawer. It's probably not totally necessary, but it'll give you peace of mind.

COPYRIGHT

Who owns your photos? You do, of course. The moment you press the shutter release button, you own the copyright to that image. To get even more protection, you can register your photos for a fee with the U.S. Copyright Office in Washington, DC, at copyright.gov. Registered or not, nobody has the right to use your images without your permission.

Copyright.gov   About Us   News

Register
Register a Copyright

GLOSSARY

APERTURE

The opening in the lens that lets light pass through to the image sensor. The aperture is usually adjustable, and measured in f-stops.

CROPPING

Using image enhancement software in the digital darkroom to eliminate unwanted portions of an image, leaving only the most important part of the scene. Cropping is a powerful way to focus attention on your subject.

DEPTH OF FIELD

A range of distance (depth), from back to front, that is in sharp focus in your scene. A "shallow" depth of field has a very narrow range of sharp focus. It is seen most often with telephoto lenses when using large apertures (such as f/2.8), and is a useful technique for blurring distracting background clutter from your images.

DIGITAL NOISE

Noise is a collection of digital artifacts, which look like clumps of grains of sand that aren't really part of the scene. It occurs most often in low-light situations where the camera sensor is set with a high ISO number.

DIGITAL SINGLE LENS REFLEX (DSLR)

A digital single lens reflex camera is a kind of camera that features interchangeable lenses and sophisticated electronics. It captures images on a digital image sensor instead of film.

F-STOP

A number that is used to tell the size of a lens's opening, or aperture. Small numbers, such as f/2.8, represent a large aperture. Small apertures, which let in less light, include f/16 and f/22.

IMAGE SENSOR

The electronic device inside a digital camera that converts light into electronic signals, which are then processed and stored on a memory card.

ISO NUMBER

A number that describes a camera sensor's sensitivity to light. Cameras that can shoot with high ISO numbers can capture images in very dim lighting conditions. The name ISO is the abbreviation for the International Organization for Standardization, a Swiss company. ISO is not an acronym for the company name. It is the root of the Greek word *isos*, which means "equal." It is pronounced "EYE-so."

MANUAL MODE

An exposure setting that lets the photographer choose both the shutter speed and the lens aperture. Today's DSLRs have extremely accurate built-in light meters. Manual mode today is used in special circumstances where control is needed, such as shooting scenes at night.

MEMORY CARD

After an image has been captured and processed by a digital camera, it is stored on a memory card, which is a solid-state storage device similar to a USB flash drive. Memory cards come in various speeds and storage capacities. Many can hold hundreds of images.

ONLINE RESOURCES

Booklinks
NONFICTION NETWORK
FREE! ONLINE NONFICTION RESOURCES

To learn more about fashion photography, visit abdobooklinks.com. These links are routinely monitored and updated to provide the most current information available.

INDEX

3/ 36

4/22 ⊙
5/25 el